Thoughts Beneath the Stars

Shugar

Copyright © 2018 Shugar

All rights reserved. No part of this book may be used or reproduced in any manner without the written permission from the author except for the use of brief quotations in a book review or scholarly journal.

Printed in the USE

www.lifecoachingthatworks.com & www.happyhikersfitness.com

All rights reserved.

ISBN-13: **978-0-692-12133-7**

CONTENTS

DEDICATIONS vii

Introduction ix

   A Trail 1

   SPIRIT 2

   Who I am Today 6

   Stone cold sober 9

   No promises 10

   I'm at the top 11

   Untitled 12

   Chances 14

   Longing for… 15

   Silence is golden 16

   Let it happen 18

   If only you could see me for me 20

   Everlasting 21

   Earth 22

   Contemplation 23

   The Love of the Oak 24

   Smile 25

   Do you hear it? 27

   Unpredictable 29

   Ocean Love 31

   One day you will find me waiting on top of the hill 32

   Reality awaits 34

LOVE	35
Take time to acknowledge it	36
Help me feel you	37
New Day - New Beginnings	41
An Angel in my presence	43
I think I want you just for myself	44
Fly Free Be HAPPY	45
Higher	46
The power of you	48
This	49
The power of the NOW	50
Keep silent	52
My SPIRIT is freer today	53
Birth	55
Don't Judge	56
Time to move forward	59
Hope	61
Spirit and LOVE...Wins Every time!	62
Birth Connections are strong	63
People come in and out of our lives	64
It's been many moons!	66
Your still here	67
Together	69
Fight on seems to be the new theme these days	70
Child	73
Death	76

Change	78
For there is a miracle happening here	79
Let's Talk	80
Oneness	82
Silence	83
Human Touch	85
I can help if you would just let me in…	86
I'm right here	89
Acceptance	91
Why am I here	94
living in the now is the way to go	96
My Wish	97
2 SOULS 2 WORLDS	99
Let's enjoy	101
Nights are hard	102
Universal Strength	103
Empowerment	104
feel you	105
A wish	107
Truth is…	110
Open your heart and just let it in	112
So, take the time to hear the silence	113
To My Child	114

DEDICATIONS

To Jessi, Danny and Zach I hope you enjoy, I LOVE you guys! You inspire me daily!
Thank you, Nature and Mother Earth, my companions through many long hours of writing and epiphanies.
To my friends who encouraged me to get this done. You know who you are...
To all those who may say.... Nothing written in this book follows Poetry "rules", welcome to my world - enjoy reading outside of the box!
Cheers to true PEACE, HOPE, LOVE and HAPPINESS

May you find peace and beauty in the following pages and may they remain with you throughout your life's journey. Warmest thoughts and best wishes across your world and with your family and friends!

INTRODUCTION

Deep in the forest on a trail, far off the beaten path, where the silence is deafening, and the mysteries of life clarify; it is there that my mind roams free of the stress of civilized existence to flow with the wind through the trees; to connect to the earth atop a falling leaf, and to contemplate...

It is in these following pages that you will find a collection of poems that reflect such journeys I have taken. Deeply personal journeys to share with you individually, yet for all to enjoy.

In these poems, I speak of LOVE and Loss, HAPPINESS and Pain, and the words pour straight from my HEART with the random purpose of...

Moving you.

Provoking you.

Helping you to open your HEARTS and minds to the HOPE and LOVE that is everywhere around us and within us.

Sometimes it takes a concerted effort to set aside our pressing concerns and listen to the JOY and LOVE that lies within our HEARTS. Let's make that effort, today, together.

Enjoy

A Trail

It's like a puzzle

Laying right in front of me
Made up of fallen leaves and shadows
Oh, how will it change your world?
If you just let it in...

Take a walk

Touch the dirt upon your feet
Smell the clean air
Feel the sun hit you upon your skin
See the beauty, all around

Seize the moment

Think about what you experience
Imagine the possibilities, if all were so lucky
Dream of a better world
Where all can see the puzzle

Put the pieces together

A world full of nature
A life full of unconditional LOVE
A journey, fun filled with adventures
An awareness of what it is like, to truly be free!

Live Free for you to just BE

SPIRIT

Let yourself BELIEVE
That you deserve it all
No matter what others may say
Because you are worth it

Giggle away your life
Cry a few tears
Clear your soul of guilt
For the world is in your hands

We are all here for a reason
At this point in time
To spread our personal message
To help others along their path

Hold onto LOVE, not guilt
Strengthen your SPIRIT, don't let it die
For these are all we truly have
To show who we really are

Look for the good in everything
Throw out the garbage around you
Confront the fears and you will be FREE
To live a beautiful life

Thoughts Beneath the Stars

Let yourself SHINE
For no matter what is going on
We can always go higher
If we just allow ourselves to do so

Fly FREE like a bird
Sore, like your light as a feather
Glide, like a leaf along the top of water
And hold your head up high like
YOU OWN THE WORLD

Fly SPIRIT, fly free

You lift me up
I thank you for that!

I want to meet you at the top
Will you wait?

I promise to catch you
If you fall....

You teach me a plethora
Thank you again

I've made mistakes
You have taught me to learn from them

I always feel your honesty
Can you accept mine?

I will hold out my hand
To help with forgiveness

Will you take it?
If not, it's ok I have more to learn!

I hold space in my HEART for you
With the goal of HAPPINES and FRIENDSHIP

For I will dream for you
When you can't
I will spread your kindness
Even after your gone

Life is more POWERFUL now
That I have learned your ways

Do you feel the same?
If not, it's ok!

Let's dream a dream together
Even if we go our different ways

For all we have is the NOW
So, let's take advantage
Time to live in the NOW

Who I am Today

I don't think I ever said THANK YOU
And I now know it's never too late...
Despite the miles between us

I remember it all
I now know
WHO I AM

No one but us will ever know
The impact you made on me
But I finally figured out, that doesn't matter

I remember,
You stated –
Just continue to be
WHO I AM

Who knew... Cereal could be for dinner?
It didn't matter what food it was
It was always just enough
To feed the stomachs and souls of all

I remember,
You made me
Learn to be the awesome chef for both bodies and souls
WHO I AM

Showing me how to make room for another
At any time of the day or night
Teaching me not to judge others ever
Take a stray in here or there, never really matters when
It always comes back 10-fold

I remember,
You taught me
To be the friend
WHO I AM

Unconditional LOVE you practiced
Forgiving, you showed me how to do
Putting your friends and family before you always
It is how I live my life now

I remember,
You showed me
The loving caring person
WHO I AM

I fight for the less fortunate
I help all I can
I teach those who ae willing to be open
I listen when someone speaks
Because I want to help

I remember,
You demonstrated to me
To always help others because it's...
WHO I AM

Respect is always important you said
As everyone is entitled to opinions
You taught me to make someone else smile
For they might need it to get through the day
We all have ups and downs
Crying and laughing along the way

I remember,
You explained
Always be there for others and to share
WHO I AM

So, as I sit by your side today
It brings me back to all my great memories
Of the things you taught me
Though our time together

I remember all the teachings,
You stated, you made, you taught, you showed,
and you explained
Because you molded me into
WHO I AM TODAY

Dedicated to my grandmother: I wrote this as I laid next to you, on my back, staring up at the sky... she really helped mold me into the person I am today!

Stone cold sober

It's worth it -
Joy filled moments
Terror in eyes....
Loneliness in the soul....
Heaviness in the stance....
LOVE in every breathe!
Happiness peaks through your lips!
Calm in your HEART!
PEACE is here, shared between us...
Please see me!
It's worth it... I promise

No promises

I cannot promise you everything
But I can offer you my all

I cannot promise you jewels
But I can offer to share my possessions

I cannot promise you smiles
But I can offer you mine to share with the world

I cannot promise you travel
But I can offer to take you to places you've never seen before!

I cannot promise to know your path
But I can offer to help pave it

I cannot promise you perfection
But I can offer you hard work, stepping up and growth from deep within

So.... I know with certainty I can and do promise...you our world

Filled with the truth, LOVE and adventure... around every corner unconditionally filled with giggles, tears, smiles, admiration, space, growth and happiness... the possibilities are endless if we just believe in each other

(Ttepol)

I'm at the top

One day you will come find me
I'll be the one waiting at the top
Smiling and giggling away
I go up there to find our strong connection
football in hand
To the way I wish it to be
I'll wait for you

Memories made in the Mountains stay in our Hearts Forever!

Untitled

Nobody's perfect
But some come close
Soaring like an Angel thru life
Despite all that is thrown

We all have our stuff
We can always do better
But if we look at the good in all
You will soon see, most are close to their awesomeness

No judgements or expectations
Just a smile here or a hand held out there
Unconditional acts are the way we should all act
To show our gratitude

For we are all, doing this thing we call life
Whether we like it or not...
So why not make the best if it
And learn to come together as one

Truth, acceptance, entitling others to their opinions

It's all part of the game

Smiling or sharing a giggle with a stranger
It too, is part of the journey
It doesn't cost a thing to do it

So, smile away
Share a giggle
Lend a hand to another
As you to will be
An Angel

Chances

I am drawn to pick a cotton ball
just once before I die
From the fields that feel so far away
Yet in reality, are oh so close

We crossed paths once, long ago
Yet I did not take the chance
Even though they were calling to me
Like an unknown trail, afraid to be taken

Silly really, the power I give
To a cotton ball in a field
But reality is, it is no different
Than any other life choice I make

I forget sometimes the signs are there
I don't take the time to acknowledge
To think of things I have let go by
All because, it did not make sense at the time

I now have learned to accept the gifts I am shown
I am willing to experience it all

Yet I find myself drawn, to the one thing I did not do
Which was to pick a simple cotton ball from that field
which I am sure was a sign from someone saying,

"I LOVE you"

Longing for...

I want to feel your laughter in my soul
When we can giggle so long
it imprints upon our hearts....

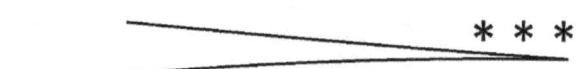

Silence is golden

Silence is golden

For it is very powerful
Life changing
In a plethora amount of ways

Look around in silence and you can **hear**

Watch leaves floating through the air, without an obstacle in their way, and hear them feed the earths platform for all to walk on

Watch the trees and **hear** them releasing oxygen to help all living things breathe

Watch some water running through natural filters and **hear** it releasing the toxins through the moss to help quench your thirst

Look at the sun releasing its warmth and **listen** to all those who enjoy

How powerful is that?

Listen carefully and you can **hear** through it
Your thoughts engaging with solutions
Your HEART beating to the beat of an excited drum
Your smile moving to the reaction of your HAPPINESS

Your LOVE for others bouncing around like an uncontrollable child running through a pumpkin patch

Incredible

It's amazing what you can hear through the silence

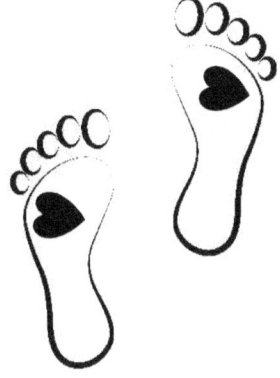

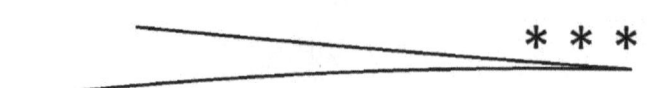

Let it happen

Try it for a moment
Go on you can do it
Close your eyes and just be...

Be the wall and you will **feel** the strength it takes to hold up a building;
Be a piece or two of grass and you will **feel** the softness it supplies to your feet when you walk upon it, over and over;
Be the wind and you will **feel** all the lyrics it carries from one place to another, as far or as close as it can reach;
Be the planet and know it doesn't matter what you do to it, it constantly evolves to keep supplying what we need to survive

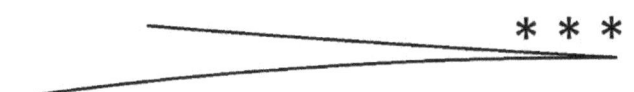

I release you into the wind

Today I sit on top of the mountain
Where I first felt you long ago
We shared a giggle, a smile and a tear that time, do you remember?
But then we moved on...
This time on the mountain alone I am reminded
Through my own smile and tears
That I still have feelings for you
Stronger and more focused just the same
I release my love for you into the wind
I will learn to wait until our paths cross again
The universe will blow you back to me when the time is right!
At which time we will once again sit on top of the mountain, to giggle, smile and shed a tear
But this time together and with the future in mind...

If only you could see me for me

Full of fun
Lovin Life
Searching for smiles
Always playing

Why don't you see

I am me always
Willing to make things work
Reaching for the gold
Enjoying every day to the fullest

Even when life throws curves

I try daily to get your attention
I go out of my way to make you smile
I lift you up
Tell you how great you are

I ask nothing in return

Everlasting

The snow falling is like a memory
The beauty and fun may only last a minute or two
But the effects are everlasting.

ttepol

Earth

As I sit here on the trail
With the wind running thru my hair
I realize how lucky we are
To have nature so close by

A tree is giving me support for my back
The river supply's me with hydration
The berry trees, they give me treats, I LOVE to eat
All while the dirt, the grass and the earth
Lift my spirits to new heights

I can't believe many hours have passed
Since I sat down on this hill
But to be honest, it feels so good
To just be part of it all

EARTH brings me food and water
With shelter and sustainability
The least I could do is sit here awhile
And be respectful of it all

I listen to the sounds moving around this space
Now I can understand
Why it is important for us all
To respect and give back to her

Contemplation

I sat today where we once sat together
Where we giggled and shared a tear
I remember it like it was yesterday
The memory is oh so strong
We have traveled many miles since then
Both together and far apart
But somehow I am always
Drawn back to that moment
When I first felt you to the core
Today as I sat in the canyon
I feel you have slipped away
It is today I accept that I must release you
Into the wind, to fly free...

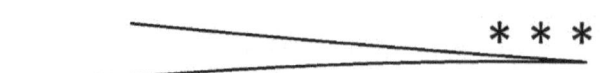

The Love of the Oak

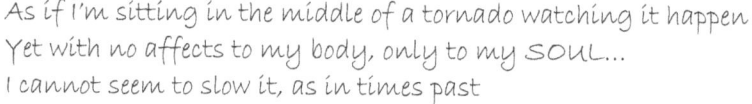

As I sit here under a big Oak tree
I can feel its power
Beauty and truth,
filled with sadness
But, somehow calming to my SOUL

The earths pull just keeps spinning
and spinning
Getting STRONGER with each
passing minute
As if I'm sitting in the middle of a tornado watching it happen
Yet with no affects to my body, only to my SOUL...
I cannot seem to slow it, as in times past

I close my eyes, I try to see
With my deepest feelings, what it is I am supposed to figure it out...
Yet there is nothing, but the sound of the wind blowing and the leaves
floating to the ground

I pause to meditate under the big Oak
For what seems, like an eternity
Three breaths in and I'm floating above the earth
Through the most vibrant of colors that only a truly special SOUL could
experience

Smile

It costs nothing,
    but it's worth a lot

It enriches those who receive it;
    without impoverishing those who give it

It happens in a flash;
    buts the memory of it sometimes lasts forever

It creates happiness in the home, fosters good will in business;
    It is the sign of friendship

It is rest to the tired, daylight to the discouraged, sunshine to the sad;
    and nature's best way to fix trouble

Yet, it cannot be bought;
    begged, borrowed or stolen

For it is something that is no earthly good to anybody;
    until it is given away

No one is so rich;
    that he gets along without it

And no one so poor;
    to not benefit from it

But if I am too troubled, sad or discouraged;
    to give you a smile

Will you please be kind enough;
    to leave me one of yours....

For nobody needs;
    A SMILE so much

As those who have none left to give

Do you hear it?

Shhh, listen carefully now
To the pitter patter of the steps
He leaves along the way

Wait for me momma
Hold my hand dadda
Wait for me peeeeeeze
As he runs to catch up

Do you see the poison oak
Look at the deer patches
See the chicory momma
No snakes dadda?
He says along the way

A giggle here
A cry there
A smile that comes from pure laughter
I can tell he loves nature
As he sings along the way

We are almost to the end
So he lays down to say, I'm tired
Hold me momma
Pick me up dadda
As we continue to walk along

Shugar

Here we are, I say
Time to go home
No he states, with a big smile
I want more

So, do you hear it now
Can you guess what it is
Full of fun and curiosity
With no judgements or preconceptions
Just full of joy in the moment...

It's the HEART and SOUL of a child
Just being
For one moment In time, himself
Which is in us all if we allow

This is dedicated to Rain who I love to the moon and back...

Unpredictable

Let's run wild in the moonlight
    under the stars
Let's feel the sand
    beneath our toes
Let's hear the sound of the water
    as it ripples through time
Let's touch each other's hearts
    forever!

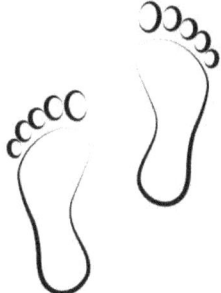

Shugar

I know you don't think it's true
But I feel your pain
I feel your laughter and your LOVE
I feel your footsteps

I have never walked on your path
But believe me when I say.... I get it
How is that possible you may ask
We all walk our own path, but, know they are sometimes similar

I'm not sure why I feel you so strong right now
The feeling inside of you is defining to the core of my being

But I know your scared
I will wait as long as it takes....

Ocean Love

she rolls in
she rolls out
without a care in the world
her beauty is like no other
she does not shrug
or push you away
embracing like no other
it's how she states
I LOVE you for you
No matter what baggage you may carry

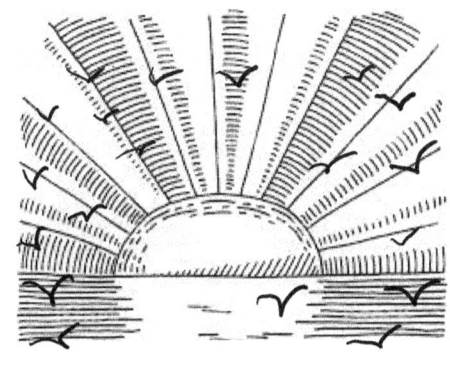

life is just here, to be lived to the fullest
just like the sun rises and sets without a thought
why the moon lights the path to greatness for all who seek it
I have a wish for humanity
And it is a very simple one
LIVE each day without judging
embrace others like you want to be embraced
don't judge for you have not walked in their shoes

just LOVE and help light the path
stand up for you and those who need a lift up
for we will all be better off
I know today will be full of LOVE which is all we can ask

who knows what tomorrow will bring
but if we are lucky
it will be like today all over again....
Lucidly LOVING and teaching PEACE

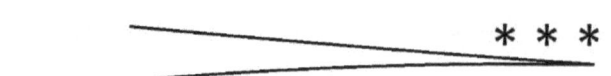

One day you will find me waiting on top of the hill

Smiling and giggling away
I go up there to find a strong connection,
football in hand
To the way I wish it to be

Giggle and laughter
Some tears, but not many
Goals and dreams being set
All While knowing
unconditional LOVE for each other
Is ready to carry us thru,
as friends to the next step

Earth is fun most times
a joke, a bad one, all the same
So, it's on top of the hill where I can vision
My next existence

Let's keep moving forward
Getting to know each other day by day
Helping each other rise
All while keeping "this" in mind

Your soul and mine
Are meshing together as one
Let the words ME and YOU vanish into...
YOU and I forever :)

Reality awaits

I want to share me with you
I hope you can do the same
This is real right?
Please tell me if it isn't

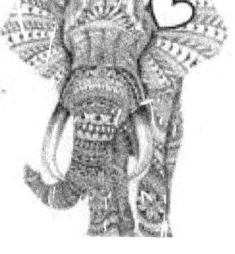

"All that we are is the result of what we have thought. The mind is everything. What we think we become."

LOVE

Hear it?
Feel it?
Embrace it...
LOVE it...

The sun rises and sets
The wind blows and
The sea rolls
All with little notice by most

If most only knew...
How much effort it takes
Yet it seems effortless to some

Imagine...
How much time it takes to get it right
Yet it passes in a split second

Let it in
Feel it change you
Nurture it and
Share it

LOVE has no limits
There are no rules
All right no wrong
For it just IS

Take time to acknowledge it

Learn from it
Teach it to others
For in its purest form
It is freedom

Free from judgements
Free from fear
Free from anger
Free from expectations...

It just IS..... ♡
Shugs

Help me feel you

Help me feel you
Hear you
See you
Different than our last encounter
oh God please!

I find it hard
I struggle to deal
I know your here
But I cannot feel

I'm sorry, I struggle
You taught me not to
I can't help it
I try to move forward

A hundred words can't bring you back
I know, because, I've said them
A million tears can't help either
I know, for I have shed them

I think about you all the time,
And it hurts every day
I hide the tears falling constantly,
My heart hurts all the time
I think about forgiveness
I even thought I saw you today

So much I can't explain
All the times I remember

Shugar

May have heard you complain
But I know you did not mean it

Hearts were broken
The day you chose to go home
It appears each one of us
Might have been left to survive alone
Is that the lesson?

I know there was a reason
That you had to leave
But keep the kids in your watchful eye please
I know it's a lot to ask
But do it
All while playing with the angels please

Fly free
Play hard
Enjoy all the LOVE
And filter it downward so we can learn from it

Mother Earths Lesson

I watch her roll
I watch her break
I admire her color
I admire her calm
I listen to her sounds

Something is different at this moment
Than from days gone past
Today I hear her talking to me directly,
loud and full of passion

Allow growth and learning she says
Allow yourself to rise above it all
Force a laugh and force a loud giggle
Allow those happy thoughts

So no matter how hard it seems
I listen with an open HEART
I do as I'm told...

I force that smile upon my face
I find something to laugh about
I mimic the giggles I hear

I find myself contemplating,
to find what she is teaching me
It is hard, but I continue
for what seems like an eternity
Forcing myself to listen
Forcing myself to smile
Forcing the giggles and the laughs

And then I hear it
I feel it
I experience it
Like a falling tree in the forest

It hits me....

My smile, after seeing a rainbow for the first time
My joy, after hearing an awesome song, you know the kind... you get up and start dancing to, even when nobody's there
I giggle so hard, I need to pee, all because I heard a silly joke

So, what is IT she wanted me to hear?

I am awesome
I am loving
I am silly and fun and chill
I am a good friend
Best of all....
I am worth it

New Day - New Beginnings

As the sun greets me upon my face
I feel it's warm touch in my life
Happy things being sent my way
And a peaceful moment takes over

Time to get moving
To start the day
With all its tests and craziness
I can do it
I know I can
No matter what is sent my way

Remember how the sun greeted me
So warm and full of life
I hope to do that to someone else today
For no other reason than I can

Sharing smiles and happiness
Is just one part of my day
To help someone else know....
To really know....
A New day, brings new beginnings
Full of hope and giggles and happiness
To be shared with all

Just like the sun did with me today!!

I see you, the real you
I feel your goodness
I hear you thru your laughter
I sense something special happening here ♡

An Angel in my presence

My HEART is pounding
Wanting out of my chest
To show all the LOVE I have to share
Because of a simple gesture, of unconditional acceptance!

I know it will never happen
I will never express how deep it runs
But I can continue, knowing
I am forever changed

I've learned to smile
I've been able to giggle
I do not have to hold back
Enlightening!

I embrace the respect, I am shown
I grow from the lessons, I hear
Even when not spoken out-loud
I am better off for having been blessed with the presence
Of a true angle that walks on this earth!

People listen
Really understand
Angels show in all forms
In all situations and
Each and every day
Be the lucky one and listen to your HEART
You will know it, when it comes
You will be changed forever,
I know....

I will never be the same!

I think I want you just for myself

But I will share you with the world
For everyone deserves to feel the way I do when around you

Happiness
Hopeful
Excited
Alive
UNCONDITIONAL LOVE

\

Fly Free Be HAPPY

You chose to fly
I understand why
I know you're feeling free
I'm glad you're living your journey!

Can you visit me sometime?
I would like that very much
I'm scared I may not feel you
I will try to be open

I talk to you still
hoping for answers
Because I want too

I try to keep moving forward
Hoping for closure
Because you asked me too

Invite me to fly with you
After a long day here on earth
just to be near each other
If only in a daughter's dream

How do we do this
I'm stuck here
You flying free
Let's help each other figure it out
Let's both fly free

Higher

Giggle and laughter
Some tears but not many
Goals and dreams being set
All While knowing
unconditional love available for each other
To lift us higher

No words needed to talk to you
For I can see you
No sounds needed to hear you
For I can feel you

I can tell you my stories
I will listen to yours
For we only have the here and now
To create "this" in the absolute!

It's ok to be scared
Its ok to chill or worry
As long as it comes from our heart and soul
We should not question **_"this"_**

I want happiness for us both
Let's let go of preconceived ideas
Then we can become everything
All that is great and meaningful!

The power of you

Teach me
Come on, you can do it
One string at a time
Please

I've always wanted to learn
To make the sounds, that make others
Both Laugh and cry
With HAPPINESS attached

So come on teach me
To hear the sounds
To feel the notes
To laugh and cry, both at the same time

How powerful it is
To hold that ability in your hands
To change someone in a split second
To make smiles instantly

All with the tools held in your hand

This

I awake with you in mind
Excitement and smiles follow
I can't wait to finish the day
So, we can talk in person

It's like a new world has begun to open up
A plethora of feelings rush thru my body
Ideas popping in my head all the time

I can't wait for the next adventure
I long for that next kiss
I look forward to creating a future
With you my love...

The power of the NOW

I'm stuck
I'm not moving forward
I find it hard to breathe
I want to cry

I find life is hard
It is a lot of work
It's hard to step forward
I hate that I am a product of my past

I find myself looking
For that point when things change
From struggling to step forward
To striving for more....

Today when I awoke
It was brought to my attention
My past makes me who I am today
But my NOW makes me who I am tomorrow

Today I giggle a little
I found myself smile once
I had a single happy thought
I dreamt a dream.

What changed, you ask
I met an angel in human form
Who showed me it's ok to just be

Thoughts Beneath the Stars

I'm allowed to feel
To cry
To laugh
To dream.

It's ok to ask for help
It's chill to just hang
It's fun to challenge yourself
It's awesome to be me

I can go to the top
stay there all day
For I am me, myself and I

I may not be perfect
I may have needs
But that's cool
Cause it makes me who I am

I am a giver
I am a friend
I am a lover
I am a dreamer

join me
On this journey on earth
Let's laugh and play and giggle and say....

Today is the first day of the rest of our lives....
Let's embrace the past and live in the now
Create a future

So bring it on
Throw it all at me
For I can take it
Because I am STRONG!

I AM ME

Keep silent

I am on fire
I will be quiet

Love has spoken
It's teaching me,
To sit back and listen

I want to hear it
I long for the fantasy
I want the child like dream

Love comes quick
Love comes in a hurry
Love is elusive

It came unexpectedly
Without me looking for it
But this time I heard it

I promise to never let go
For the fight for us
Is worth everything...

Love is... you and I forever

My SPIRIT is freer today

I feel like flying
I want to shout to the world
I don't ever want this to go away!
I feel spiritually free

Why today...
I have no idea...
Could it be the beautiful blue sky
The roars of the breaking ocean water

I have no idea...
Possibly the LOVE in my HEART,
Coincidently the new-found Freedom of being me

I don't know... and I don't care
Feeling spiritually free feels great
Who cares why
I'm going with the flow

I'm following my path
The winds start to blow a little harder
My HEART beats a little faster
By smile reaches news peaks

My eyes shine a bit more
I realized today this has always been possible
I just would not let it happen
For happiness changes your world
You see good all-around

LOVE heals
And laughter will
Set you free

So today I say
Allow it to be
Live in the now and
Set yourself loose
To be

Spiritually free

Birth...

I hear her calling,
 through the wind
I see her when,
 I close my eyes
I can feel her touch me,
as I sit on a hill
I do not understand this
As we have never met
All my life
 I felt this way
When I was young
I used to dream
Could she LOVE horses
as much as I
Does she like
the outdoors
Is family time as special to her
As much as it was to me?
I wondered about these things for years
Why I am not sure
I am told we are molded
by those around us every day
And by our
surroundings and explorations
But I always felt there was one more factor
Which is that of our birth cells

Don't Judge

As I sit here looking down at my pink hair
I cannot help but wonder,
What others might think or even say
Even though they don't know me

I am fun and sensitive and will bend over backwards
For anyone with a need or two
I might even share a laugh or a song
Just to help lift up your mood

I can cook and grow food, for all to enjoy
I can make a mean dessert,
Believe it or not
I can even take those who are open
Into nature to find a little more to life

But none of this will be possible
if you don't give me the time of day
To share all my strengths, fun and joy
So go ahead and maybe give me half a chance
To show you who I am

Thoughts Beneath the Stars

Pink hair, obese, skinny or not, is the "norm"
These should never be a factor
Go on
try it
say hi, just because
Who knows you may just find the laughter

The laughter that helps you through that hard day
Or get you thru a hard time in life
And move you forward to take your next step
Without judgements or regrets

Don't judge or give me a cold shoulder
because I don't fall into normalcy
And I promise you will not regret it ever
For I will always be there for you my friend! No regrets

Thank you for finding me
Thank you for being you
Thank you allowing us to be:)

Time to move forward

Why do I hold myself back
I may never know
It's hard work though
So maybe I should just let go

Allow myself to win
To feel the pats on the back
To tell what I have accomplished
Yes, I should just let go

It hits me again
Like a ton of bricks
Allow myself freedoms and wins
I'm not sure I'm worthy
Maybe I should let go

Will I feel encouraged
Can it be fun
I think I shall try it, if only for a moment
I should let go

Shugar

Ok off I go, to allow myself
To have a win
for hiking a long trail
To allow myself to smile
when I don't quit
To laugh at myself for
getting back up after that fall
Yes, I'm letting go

It feels good to smile
And laugh and sometimes
giggle at myself
Because I now know
its ok great to fail a time or two
Yes, I'm letting go

Why you ask is that good
I'm going to let myself
Win no matter how long it may take
All because I let go of expectations
And allowed myself to reach my goals

Yup I let go!

Hope

Longing again to see
Asking questions to figure it all out...
I want to feel, really, I do
Here's to finding me

Spirit and LOVE...Wins Every time!

Feel It
See it
LOVE it
Answer it

LOVE is all around
It can disappear in a minute
No shit
Really

A sunflower opens
A rose closes
The wind blows perfume
The earth shows its fangs

Allow the good in
Spit out the doubt
For it's the only way to survive
The alternative is not spiritual

One step at a time
One smile a day
One giggle an hour
One lesson a life time

Stand tall
Ride the waves
Take the time
To move in the right direction

I like to think....
SPIRIT and LOVE always wins

For its survival

Birth Connections are strong

I never understood it
I could never grasp it
I never could fully embrace it

I got the call
it was early morning
I was already up

Surprising I was not shocked by the news
An overwhelming emptiness took over
For just a split moment
I never felt deprived
As those around me filled my needs
She gave to me my family, I could not ask for more

As I just realized I could never physically connect
With the one human who gave me life
Not even for one second

I say THANK YOU

Dedicated to my birth mother I never met!

People come in and out of our lives

For no apparent reason
They push us down
They lift us up
They make us cry
They make us smile

To guide us on our path

Right way or not
They have a lesson to teach us
To hold us back or push us toward enlightenment
Always something to learn

Where does life take us?

We learn everyday
We make mistakes
We take one step forward
To take two steps back

On the JOURNEY we continue

Until we find our way
To figure out why we are here
Move forward more than back
Giggle, Laugh and learn along the way

Take a chance

Allow someone in
Allow yourself to LOVE you
TRUST in human kind and the earth

TRUST in you

It's been many moons!

I haven't felt like this is so many moons
Do you remember me like I
remember you?
The sun has risen, and the moon has set
So many times, but I will never forget

You make my world light up
I get high just thinking about you
The possibilities are endless
If we just allow the Starrs to come out!

Any interaction is fun
And true to our HEARTs

You know what I mean
I know it in my HEART!

Your still here

I can still hear you
Still feel you
Somehow see you
Can you do the same?

I thank you
I honor you
I make you proud
For you always do the same

Things change
We will adapt
Take the challenge
Let's do this together

If you want to fly
I understand
Freedom is personal
I will support your decision

For now, I will hold space
I will listen to your wishes
I will respect your choices
I will help you through this

Don't be afraid
Do what you desire
For you are in control
Enjoy your journey

I respect you
I honor you
I trust you
I LOVE you

Sleep well, say hi to Grandma and play with the angels

Dedicated to my mother.... written just moments before her death and read to her just before she decided to fly free from this place we call earth....

Together

Reach for me today
Touch our lives forever
Never beyond your grasp
Ever present for you
Fill our hearts with LOVE
Together we can just "**BE**"

Fight on seems to be the new theme these days

I promise to continue
to push on
I promise to not let the loss
always bring me down
I promise to continue
telling stories of your past
I promise to keep
your intentions afloat

I look into your eyes
I feel your heart beat
I hear your words
I see your beautiful soul – L.G.

Shugar

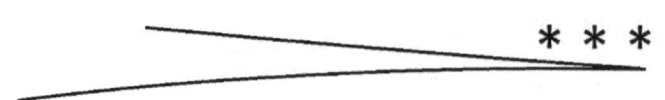

Remember Me When…. you spread the LOVE
Remember me when… you hear the wind blow
Remember me when… the light shines on your face
Remember me when…you feel the tide upon your feet
Remember me when…you bake cookies - vegan of course
I will always be here close and strong
I can hear you so LOUD, so STRONG
When you speak and when you listen you will hear me and feel my presence …
I love you sweat pea

This poem is dedicated to a starr…

Child

Listen now, Please Listen
Hear me honoring you, my child
Your memory will sometimes blur

DO NOT GIVE IN
You will hear me, you will see me

EMBRACE IT
For you are strong

Fight the fatigue
Look through the fog

Reach for your dreams
For you are strong

Please remember Please Please Please
Do not give into fear,

Embrace it
Do not succumb

Keep going...
You have lots more to do

For you are strong
Spread your Peace and LOVE

Make it your mission
Share it as if daily words for all to live by

For YOU are strong
You came to this planet

To make a difference
To help guide all children of earth

Help all do their personal best
So, they too can learn to say

You are strong
It's time to move forward

It's time to share all your LOVE and give peace
to those around, remember you can do this

You are STRONG
For we will forever be strong together in our newly combined world

For I am with you always

I LOVE you....

Contemplation
Peace
Happiness
Laughter

Keep it a bay
You will struggle for years
Allow it in for a minute
It will change you forever

Peace out:)

Death

I awaken to the silence
That your passing leaves behind
It's hurts my heart
To know this is my new forever

**I've spent many hours thinking
Shed many tears as well**

I know you meant well
I know you did your best
I know we had our troubles
I know deep down you cared
I know you did not want to go
I know it was your choice
Nothing else matters now anyway

**Because of our crazy connection
my memory banks are full**

I remember our travels
Filled with giggles and amazement
I remember our parties
So full of craziness to pull them off
I remember our conversations
Wondering how or why something was happening
I remember the good times
I have chosen to forget the rest

I want to thank you, for
Through your actions
I watched, and I learned

You taught me to fight for what I needed
I learned no one would do it for me
You taught me to never give up
I learned I could always do it myself
You taught me stand up for what I truly believe in
I learned to follow my heart
You taught me to fight rough
I learned to stand tall and brave

The future brings promise you showed me that

* * *

Change

Your soul and mine
Can be one in the same
We can do this
We got this
For we will change lives
Starting with our own

For there is a miracle happening here

I started from a seed
A single seed
With very little direction to go
I wait to see

I felt the water fill me with joy
Food brought me fullness
Light gave me energy
And the LOVE...well pure
Happiness

I take each day as it comes
I tackle it
I grow
I add color to my beingness
I gain confidence

I bloom into my own beauty
I hope to share with others
I produce smiles and things to help
I am here for the taking

I LOVE me
I LOVE you
I LOVE life
I hope to spread the LOVE

For LOVE is the end goal
Today and forever....

Let's Talk

I'll meet you in Neverland
In real time or in our sleep

Doesn't matter really
As long as we can talk

It helps me get through the day
Does it help you at all?

I often dream of HAPPINESS
I see you actually feel it

I hope for betterment
You are raising everyday

I will catch up
Can you wait?

I will be on the trail
If we meet that's great

But if we don't
I will move on

Holding onto
The hope I can rise too

If only in my dreams
To hear your voice of help

Telling me it's OK

Thoughts Beneath the Stars

I had to leave
I did not want to
It's not ideal
But we chose Baby steps

I had to go
I questioned my actions
It's not what I wanted
I remind myself to take
Baby steps

Maybe today I will stay
Even if just for one more day
It's now what I want
Baby steps are no longer on my mind

We laugh
We giggle
We kiss
We make love

You make me think
You make me question
What will become of "this"
Whatever that is?

Oneness

I want to look into your eyes while making love
I will feel your heart beating with mine
At that moment we will become one

Silence

For years I have been quiet
While on the run
But all I really wanted
Was to find some fun

So, all this time
I was searching high and low
But I was not successful
Because of being too low

Then the day came,
I got the one chance

I gave up the SILENCE I once had
During this time, I thought things would change
And the fun would take over the silence

I was right for awhile
As I found laughs and smiles
With the help of my friend
All the way to the end

I recall the good times
While on trips and walks
With my friend
Whom I like to share talk

Shugar

During this time, I was learning a lot
Including the fact, this relationship could never end
But no matter what ever happened I decided to keep
These special memories I had with my best friend
Then the day came
When the SILENCE was again upon me
But this time it was different
Why? I could not see

I now know it doesn't matter
What others will say
Cause I know what to do
To go the right way

See I had found that sometimes SILENCE was ok
As long as I never ever again would say
That when things are rough, SILENCE is the way
Cause that's no longer true now that I've decide to stay...

Human Touch

It's been years
since I felt it
But did I ever really feel it
I can't remember
the feeling it brought
Nor the emotions that followed
Did I ever really feel it? I do not know

I could imagine
it makes you smile
Maybe it gives a safety sensation
Perhaps a feeling of

living in a dream world
All which is followed by
Unconditional LOVE

One day I will feel it again, I know it
But until that day
I will live my life with the hopes
Of once again, feeling safe, with another
Knowing that
unconditional LOVE is attainable
And all because
I may connect in the future with
Someone who accepts me for me!

I can help if you would just let me in...

I feel I can't breathe
I should maybe pace myself for awhile
I feel ill and scared maybe even down?
I may not know why I feel the way I do
For its hard at first to see
But when I see it... the root reason blows

You may not know it
But I Feel your pain
I feel your heart hurt
I can absorb it....
I can help if you let me

I can't explain it
Why I can feel you
But I know deep down inside
We crossed paths for a reason

If you let me in
If you let me help
If you let me take the hurt away
You will be able to move freer

I can handle it if you open up
I can get rid of it myself
I am visiting here for the very reason
If you would just let me in

TRUST the process
Put TRUST in me, so
You can TRUST in you
Allow yourself to be free
NOW

Shugar

* * *

I promise to listen
To always speak my truth
Can you do the same
Let's see where this goes

I'm excited
Like a little kid
Do you feel it
I hope so

Speak the truth, even if your voice shakes.

-Maggie Kuhn ●

I'm right here

Please open your eyes
Allow me into your heart
I'm right in front of you
I am the greener grass on the other side

I am not perfect

I may not be dripping with money
I may be overweight
I may be insecure sometimes too
But I am always striving or more

I am here for you

Through thick and thin
I will hold your hand if you're scared
I will push you out of harm's way
I will listen to your concerns of life
I will help you get through it

I am a good person

I will stop to help someone in need
I will go out of my way to make others laugh
I will go the extra mile to see a great sunset
I will be true to the end

Shugar

No matter what happens

I can always pick you up
I will always hold out a hand
I can give you all that I have
I will always hold a in my heart for you

Always

Acceptance

We search for it our whole life

I've been searching for it,
Ever since I can remember
I've received it truly once or twice
It should not be this hard
For it should be unconditional

I am me, it's that simple
I don't ask you to be anyone else
I am full of fun and happiness
Yet some cannot see it

When younger I searched hard
Though I stuck to the accepted words
Then I stopped looking for more
To not hurt other's feelings

Now that I'm finding me again

I see that there is no norm
There's only TRUTH and HONESTY
Which are the foundations
Of a good human being

So, go ahead

I will live like there's no tomorrow
I will accept all others without expectations
All I ask in return
Accept me for who I am

Shugar

Your smile changes me
Your laughter makes me feel alive
Your ideas change my thoughts
Your love for life shows me anything is possible

Thoughts Beneath the Stars

I am a giver
I am a friend
I am a lover and
I am a dreamer

Join me
On this journey on earth
Let's laugh and play and giggle and declare....

Today is the first day of the rest of our lives....
Let's embrace the past and live in the now
And create a FUTURE

So, bring it on
Throw it all at me
For I can take it
Because I am STRONG

I AM ME.

> "Everything has changed and yet, I am more me than I've ever been" – Iain Thomas

Shugar

Why am I here

I ask myself often
Is it to live in the now
Or to build a DREAM of tomorrow

Life gets I the way sometimes

A simple task turns crazy
A giggle into a cry
A HOPE into a quest
A DREAM into a reality

It is hard to keep going

Which way is correct
I go with my gut most days
Never sure if it's spot on
But I must continue the path

Helping others is what I do

Help another see his path
Lift a human up
Get him to DREAM a DREAM
Is very satisfying

How do I help me

This is a hard task
For I am WORTH it
Where do I want to go
I am never quite sure

What I do know

Is to help others is to help me
For it brings me HAPPINESS
I HOPE just once along this path
I too find a hand to pull me along

Shugar

living in the now is the way to go

To experience and have fun along the way
To share this with others who have similar goals
It's more than EMPOWERING

It makes **life EPIC** and **COMPLETE**
Thanks to you all!!

My Wish

Wish we could spend time just as 2 SOULS together at play
No earthly judgements
For if you could just see me
You could learn a lot, perhaps

I maybe rough on the outside
But that's not who I am
I am me, fun loving, spirited and full of life
Please don't let my outside scare you

I know it's hard to get past
But maybe one day you will accept
My outer shell tells a story....

I have personally been through death and back
I have listened and absorbed stories one could only pray never to hear
I have stared death in the eyes
I have watched others give up
I have seen true disappointment lead to despair
I have seen, LOVE turn to hate
Yet I am still here

Some may wonder why I keep going
Despite what I have seen and heard and lived
Yet I am still here

Shugar

So, check this out
My inner self tells a story too
I have gone from the bottom to the top and back to the bottom
Yet I am on my way up again
I have cried till I released enough to smile from ear to ear
I have traveled the world over to see its beauty and all it has to give
I have given birth to 3 humans who have great souls and I'm honored they chose me
I have laughed through thick and thin
And yet I am still here
Loving life fully

So maybe one day you can put aside my outer shell
And look back at me to say....
I see you for you!

2 SOULS 2 WORLDS

I am not afraid to LOVE you
I am afraid of not being loved back

There are words, I know you LOVE to hear
I know I will never hear from you

Don't be so distant, as to not listen
I feel the words in my HEART anyway

Being in LOVE is not what makes me HAPPY
It is the person I LOVE that does

I see the SPIRIT in your eyes
You make me fall to my knees

Sometimes I feel we can read each other's thoughts
But I cannot find the words to express how I feel

I can always find a way to understand you
Yet, I find it hard for you to really see me

Because of outside influences
Most days are confusing but encouraging

It is hard to stay steady on this path
For I know it could lead somewhere, maybe...

Shugar

But together we could be great, if we just give it a try... no
EXPECTATIONS

Sometimes I wonder but mostly I know for sure
What you are thinking and feeling

Yet I fail to communicate the true SPIRIT thoughts
For I do not want you to bail 100% for another way

I BELIEVE so strongly in us and all that we have shared
We cannot go any further the way we are

I realize I need you to just be there
Lover, friend or distant acquaintance

I cannot fix the way I feel
Just to keep me grounded

I wish you could see it
To remind me I'm not that way off

Just know that
My HEART belongs to you

Our SOULS will become one
One Lifetime soon

I will continue to believe that
I must for my soul's survival

Let's enjoy...

Let me hold you when you need
Let me wipe away the tears
Let me support you to the fullest
Everything will work out

I ask for nothing in return
Don't ask why
Enjoy our ride together
For it is just ours...
we have found our "this"

Peace

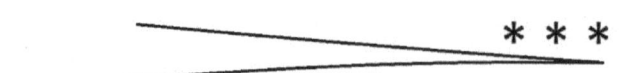

Nights are hard

Memories flare strong
The sight of those last moments
I must hide the tears

I can't move beyond them
I try with all I have
I have nowhere to turn
My heart is on fire

I'm told it gets easier
I'm told to let the sadness flow
I'm told a lot of things
But I'm alone at night to deal

Universal Strength

I can feel the rising of the sun it brings me calmness,
even when it retires at night

I can feel the blowing of the wind it makes me feel alive,
when there is a chill in the air

I see the opening of flower buds
which brings me thoughts of starting again

I see the blue in the sky, anytime of the year,
which makes me feel all warm inside

I hear the rustling of leaves falling, I am instantly reminded
change is always happening

It is nice to feel and see that beauty
surrounds us at all times

It resembles STRENGTH and LOVE
and PEACE that the universe provides
Asking NOTHING in return!

Empowerment

Adventure awaits
Creativity will come
Let's take a chance
It's worth the risk

feel you

As I listen to your voice
I can't help but reaffirm
How talented you are

I see you

I can hear it with my eyes
I can imagine it with my ears
I can touch it with my HEART

I hear you

The DREAM maker
You are the finisher
The conductor for all to capture their personal HAPPINESS

I Laugh with you

What you do is like no other
You can make someone cry
Or smile with just a pull of a string

I cry HAPPY tears with you

You raise me up
You teach me to DREAM
You show me how to LOVE

I become more of me when your around

Thank you for your talents
I'm grateful for it all
I HOPE I can repay you

Our friendship grows in the now
Our souls will continue to connect stronger every Lifetime
Until we both understand our strength together and create as
ONE

A wish

Not sure if you know this
But I feel you everyday

When you are hurting
I cry a tear
When you are HAPPY
I giggle out loud

I hope you see
That I wish for you to be HAPPY

When you are smiling
My HEART beats a little faster
When you are laughing
I am in a state of bliss
Funny how we came together
As strangers at first

I knew the first time I heard about you
You were SPECIAL

I'm lucky enough to spend time with you
To see firsthand the gifts, you have to offer

My only DREAM for you

Shugar

Is for you to know you
You are an ANGEL on earth
Sent to spread LOVE and HAPPINESS
You lift people up constantly
You get people to DREAM for a better life

Please take the time to enjoy you
And to allow others to complete you

For you deserve the best there is to offer
Every hour of every day
For I believe if you let it happen
You will see your life move forward at warp speed

Rise to the occasion
For it should be celebrated

Come one come all
Meet the new NGEL on earth
Who can help us ALL see
That life is special for all to enjoy

Thank you for being you
Thank you for helping us rise up
Thank you for sharing your WISDOM
That you for allowing us on your path
Thank you for getting me to see mine

My wish for you is to see you change the world daily with your offerings

Thoughts Beneath the Stars

Laughter is the sound I hear
So free and oh how powerful
It reminds me of my HAPPY life
And brings me back to me

Who am I you might ask
Well that's a long story to tell
But the short of it is
I am me
Bright, Beautiful, fun and free

To be who I am meant to be,
Every minute of the day
Even on days when "things" get in the way
Is an awesome journey to live
I welcome the laughter to always
Bring me back
To me

I dream and wish and travel through my thoughts
In search of what, exactly, I do not know
But I am sure I can always find a part of me
Every time I hear that sound
Of joy and HAPPINESS that comes from within

Its laughter I search for endlessly
That's seems to guide me to my HAPPY place
That makes me, the me, I am meant to be!

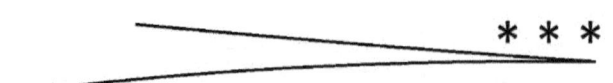

Truth is...

So, I finally told the truth today
It was like a thousand pounds off my shoulders
Yet I was greeted with disgust

I am not sure how that happens
For you have always told me to be honest
But I now understand that's not what was requested

You want me to be "normal"
Whatever that may mean
Why can't you see we all have our own normal?
That brings us HAPPINESS

I'm shocked at the response I got
For I never judged you so harshly
But that's what make us different I guess

For you see I only want you to be HAPPY
To enjoy the time, you have left on this planet
To find HAPPINESS and live in whatever way you wish

I am sad that you do not want this for me
Sure, you want me to be HAPPY but, on your terms,
You want me to find LOVE but only in the "normal" way whatever that means

Thoughts Beneath the Stars

I will abide by your wishes and wait til you die to search for LOVE
I will not resent you for your request
For I know that the day will come
That I can truly be me

I must tell you what I have learned from this
I will LOVE my kids unconditionally
I will LOVE them for who they are,
AS, I have no right to tell them who they are
I will never tell anyone they cannot be themselves
I will never suppress another's reach for HAPPINESS
I will support anyone's decision to find LOVE

For now, I understand more than ever... the search for one IDENTITY!

Open your heart and just let it in

Open your heart and just let it in
What on earth are you talking about
The world is a wonderful place
If you just let her in

Nature, Laughter, facts and fiction
Is all part of our world
To make us smile and giggle and think a little
Or maybe to teach us

How you ask
What could this teach us
I do not understand
Please explain

Growth and strength is all around us
If you just watch and learn
You will be ok

So, take the time to hear the silence

Remembering all the while
Everything has a purpose, a job, and a sound to share if you allow it

No expectations equals freedom so close your eyes, let it all in, and become, a better you

All because you let the silence in :)

Shugar

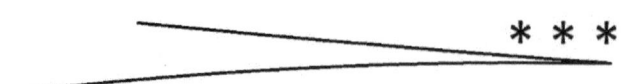

Dedicated to each of my children who I LOVE unconditionally and without you all I would not be whole:

To My Child

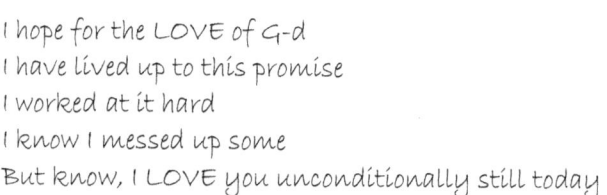

The first time I looked into your eyes
I made you a promise
Unconditional LOVE at all times
No matter what ever came up

I hope for the LOVE of G-d
I have lived up to this promise
I worked at it hard
I know I messed up some
But know, I LOVE you unconditionally still today

I remember your first cry
I held you close to my HEART
And Promised I would make it better
I think I did just that, as you smiled deeply

I remember your first day of school
You were so scared
I held you close to my HEART
And promised it would get better
It did look at where you are now

Thoughts Beneath the Stars

I remember the first time you yelled at me
SO angry, for what reason I don't recall today
I held you close to my HEART
And promised we would get through it
We did look at us now
Sharing our hopes and dreams for a better world together

I remember your first heartbreak
Your HEART was broken in two
I held you close to my HEART
And promised you would find your right match
You did I see it in your smile when you talk about LOVE

I remember your first doubt about your life
You did not know the next step to take
I held you close to my HEART
And promised I would help you find your path
You figured it out; you change people's
HEARTS daily

I remember my first wishes for you
I held you close to my HEART
And promised life would be full of fun and laughter, DREAMS attained, and HAPPINESS truly found
I think you get it
I hear your giggles, I smile at your laughter and I rise to meet you daily

My only hope now
Is that you have learned
To receive and give unconditional LOVE
Not only to others but to yourself!
Today, I hold you close to my HEART
And I promise
I am here always offering you my Child

UNCONDITIONAL LOVE ALWAYS

May the next chapter of your journey be better than the last, may it bring you all the happiness and peace you can handle, and may all your goals be reached!!!!

www.ingramcontent.com/pod-product-compliance
Lightning Source LLC
Chambersburg PA
CBHW031139090426
42738CB00008B/1147